Prison Lingo 101

by

William Malicoat

Published by

www.designedconviction.com

www.omaliart.com

I am an artist who isn't afraid to take chances on your visions, ideas or creative thoughts, and apply it to a canvas. My goal is to afford a quality painting keeping a subtle balance between two worlds, realistic and impressionistic.

Whether it is for your home, office or a gift for a loved one, give me a chance to create something for you within your budget, series paintings are also available upon request.

To my family and friends, thank you for always being there for me.

To the reader:

I hope this small glimpse into the prison world helps you better understand a few things about us and some of our acquired vocabulary.

If this book leaves you hungry for more, then prepare for an interesting read.

My journey to the Washington State Penitentiary as a young boy. This book called "The Other Side of The Game" which is a reflection upon my past and being prison bound because of my choices. You'll walk in the shoes of a boy stepping on board the prison hound and learn drastic changes and experiences prison has offered.

Written by firsthand experience by Will Malicoat and published by Design Conviction

PRISON LINGO 101

INTRODUCTION

This book is intended to help the average person on the streets better understand the crazy lingo inmates use. It's common men and women correspond with those incarcerated and language barriers may exist.

This book is inspired by my wife who continually ask's me, "what does that mean". So, I am sharing a unique world of intrigue with those who are curious about us on the inside.

Also, I have incorporated a few helpful things in case you might be on a journey for your first prison visit experience.

It's very common that people will struggle on their first visit and may have anxiety about several things even before entering the visiting room.

CHAPTER 1

Learning the Lingo

1) <u>Been Down</u>: This terminology is commonly used to reference how long we've been incarcerated.

2) <u>Fell or When I fell</u>: This is the term used to reference when we left the streets, got arrested or came to prison.

3) <u>Stateish</u>: Everything the state provides, Clothing, shoes, etc. Usually people who are referring to being broke will say, "all I have is state—ish".

4) <u>Indigent</u>: Very similar to state-ish, however people will refer to using indigent or being indigent. This is what the state gives the broke people for their hygiene. Typically, the indigent products are something you will never find in the local store for resale. It is of low quality and doesn't leave a person feeling very clean or refreshed, a sad state of affairs if your indigent.

5) <u>Soup</u>: Top Ramen is what we call soups, not the common cambe11's or progresso fancy stuff. A soup is the most common staple a person will retain at all times.

6) <u>Butt Naked Soup</u>: Because most inmates use the soup as their staple food, it becomes the partial ingredient for most "spreads". However, a butt naked soup is bare bones, eating it straight up with no extras, like beans, cheese or meat. Another indicator that your person is on broke status, if they say "I'm eating a butt naked soup".

7) <u>Pruno</u>: Another word we use for prison hooch, which is not made in toilets as people have seen on Shawshank Redemption.

8) <u>Wet Cell or Dry Cell</u>: We have different levels of security most types of cells will determine the level a person is on. Wet cells will have toilet and sink which is associated with maximum security, some institutions in Washington State have medium security units that have wet cells. The dry cells have no running water, which means you share a community bathroom. Dry cells are predominantly associated

with a lower custody, like minimum security or camps.

9) <u>Courtesy Flush</u>: When someone is taking a # 2 and they hit the button to keep the water flowing. Also, a common phrase used would be "putting some water on it". Keeping the bathroom stink to a low rumble.

10) <u>Main1ine</u>: When we get called for chow it's usually announced by unit or pod really loud "MAINLINE". Also, this term is used to determine a solid person being able to walk mainline, or they might be on "P.C." protective custody.

11) <u>P.C—Case</u>: Somebody might refer to a person as a "PC— Case meaning they pull shady moves to keep themselves isolated from the mainline which is the rest of the population.

12) <u>S.T.G.</u>: Facilities may label people who are associated with gangs as "Security Threat Groups". Once given this status it becomes harder to obtain jobs, schooling and staying under the radar.

13) <u>House Mouse</u>: A person who never leaves the cell is considered a house mouse. These guys are truly a bummer never giving the

roommate time to chill and relax in their own space.

14) <u>Fence Book</u>: Many facilities have multiple yards to do activities, some are split by chain link fences. When people congregate along the fence line it's called "Fence Book" getting all the daily gossip and drama from other units.

15) <u>Pill—Line</u>: Pills are given, usually called "ding— biscuits" at particular times. It's like a drive through window with a nurse handing out medications.

16) <u>Fee Fee</u>: This is a devise commonly made out of rubber gloves and placed in a rolled-up towel with Lotion inside. A guys toy!

17) <u>Ad—Seg or Admin Segregation</u>: Stuck in the hole pending some investigation or more than likely an infraction.

18) <u>Punk</u>: Weak minded coward who more than likely takes it in the ass or sucks dick.

19) <u>S.O.</u>: Usually we throw this verbiage around to those who are sex offenders.

20) <u>Chimo</u>: The bottom of the barrel as prison politics go the "child molester" gets no respect on mainline.

21) <u>Diaper Sniper</u>: The same as above another name we use for a child molester or one who takes advantage of little girls.

22) <u>Pop—A—Socket</u>: People in prison aren't privy to lighters or matches generally, so they will use pencil lead and Q—tips to gather the spark from arcing the wall socket. We call it "popping a socket", this gives us the flame to smoke or burn stuff.

23) <u>Stand point or Keepin point</u>: Someone who is the lookout person IS e one standing point, keeping an eye for the rats or cops.

24) <u>Getting your money</u>: This could be used two ways, one could be used in reference to hitting the gym hard and getting your money. The other is used to reference when someone is hitting a lick, rubbing one out, alone time!

25) <u>Zoom—zooms & Wham—Whams</u>: This is usually for the person who gets store and all the goodies, mostly fat boy treats and spread fixings.

26) <u>Getting Clipped</u>: Someone who is on the naughty list and owes money or some other worthy fault, is getting beat up, or as we say, "getting clipped".

27) <u>Mission Boy</u>: The guy who got clipped, is usually hit by the mission boy or the missile. He puts in work for his people to show heart and integrity proving he is solid.

28) <u>Shit Eater</u>: People call the warden and the C/O's shit eaters.

29) <u>Getting your joints ran</u>: This could be used two ways, the punk, he gets his joints ran or anybody else who

takes it in the ass. Also, this could be used like you lost so bad you got your joints ran.

30) <u>A Stick</u>: This is an extremely small joint which would make you laugh, smaller than a toothpick.

31) <u>A one-seater or two-seater</u>: This is referencing the above stick, which if super skimpy would be a one-seater, if it was fat it would be a two seater.

32) <u>Street—2—Street</u>: People who sell things or pay large debts would commonly prefer to send money via "street   .to street" My people to your people.

33) <u>Cadillac</u>: This is like a Starbucks coffee on steroids made with cocoa and candy bars, commonly made in county jails, and will have your hair standing up.

34) <u>$100 Paper</u>: This is a drug reference which indicates you get a larger amount then just buying a couple sticks. Still a fragment compared to street values.

35) <u>Shower Shark</u>: This guy is the predator who waits for the young boys to shower and finds a reason to be busy watching him shower, trying to sneak a peek.

36) <u>Peter Gazer</u>: This guy is similar to the above but takes it even further to catch you pissing sizing your package up and smiling like you're a piece of meat.

37) <u>Keester</u>: This term is used when somebody hides something in their but, you would "Keester" it, also coined the suitcase.

38) <u>A Boat</u>. In Washington State sack lunches are given in a prepackaged cardboard tray with plastic wrap over it and referred to as 'I A Boat".

39) <u>White Money</u>: When somebody in prison has real currency, it is called

"White Money". Most commonly used for trade with staff as the money is on hand.

40) <u>Meat Stick</u>: This is a hot commodity in prison, usually a meat stick would be some form of a summer sausage.

41) <u>Shit Sheet</u>: So, when people are living in a wet cell and they have a roommate, when they use the toilet to go # 2, they would apply a sheet to cover the toilet area. This is referred to as the "Shit Sheet".

42) <u>McFe10n</u>: This is prisons version of McDonalds McMuffin only ours is

much worse lacking flavor and real meat.

43) <u>Jack Shack</u>: When somebody's roommate leaves for visit or school and is gone for a long period of time, the room is considered the "Jack Shack" alone time

44) <u>A spread</u>: This is when the fellas get together and all pitch in on a big nacho or   fixing of some sort it considered a spread.

45) <u>Drop out</u>: This is when somebody was cool and more than likely had joined a gang or was affiliated with one and has dropped out.

46) <u>Green Light</u>: this is usually referred to when somebody is on hold for smashing out another person or given the "green light" to get them. This is paramount to getting people from different races, you must get the green light.

47) <u>Solid Dude</u>: This is a pretty straight forward phrase, but a solid guy is somebody with good paperwork trust worthy or down for the cause.

48) <u>Miss Move</u>: This is used when somebody screwed up, made a bad choice, or when we move somebody in our cell that is otherwise not on our page. That's a miss move!

49) <u>Catching an STD</u>: This is not a sexual disease as one would assume. It's when somebody says to come in their house or catch a heads up, and they catch an STD, "Scared to Death" they piss down their leg.

50) <u>Come New</u>: This said during a fight when one person has been faded or subdued, they say "come new" meaning start fresh round two.

CHAPTER 2

Information on Do's and Don'ts when corresponding with inmates.

1) Never assume what you see on TV is factual, when chatting with your person ask questions before leaning on assumptions.

2) When corresponding refrain from using words like punk or bitch, for a guy it would be fighting words, meaning he has been disrespected to the fullest.

3) Most commonly new attractions who don't send a picture will rarely get a response, cat fishing is real in prison.

4) Refrain about asking questions on hot topics, such as drugs or gang affiliation or personal business which could bring red flags to the institution.

5) Be very cautious when meeting somebody else 's person or people out there. When they are mutual friends with your person, drama is waiting if your not careful.

6) Be straight forward with your intentions it's easier to set boundaries in the beginning.

7) Keep it real! Earning trust on shaky ground is a deal breaker for most, obviously this is a two-way street.

8) Most people in prison are like an open book, you already know more about them then they do you, use this to your advantage.

9) When establishing phone communication, always be prepared to talk about the phone money budget, because calls will add up really fast.

10) Small messages are better than no messages. Whether it's a quick letter or email via J—Pay, it's the simple things that bring smiles usually.

11) Always be honest about your appearance or weight because you might actually meet this person one day. Also, building something real means excepting the real you or the real them.

12) Try not to share any negative feelings with your people about your person or they will be polluted with that perception you've given.

13) Try not to make assumptions and put labels on people, not everybody is the same or their crime doesn't always define them.

14) When corresponding via telephone you will need extra patience because it will randomly cut you off or give you some three—way alert when you didn't even do anything.

15) If your person's state has the J—Pay system and you intend on emailing try and add one stamp with your message so they can respond.

16) If you intend on sending a card, be cautious with using crayons, or magic

markers your person may never even receive your greeting card due to the facility thinking you 've placed drugs magically in the marker or crayons.

17) It's usually a good rule of thumb to check with your persons facility rules to see if they have anything funky that could reject your mail, phone calls or emails.

CHAPTER 3
Preparation for first visit and what to expect

1) Bring an extra outfit in case the visiting room dress code is crunchy about you being too sexy.

2) Find out beforehand whether your persons facility uses cash or change

or card or keys for the vending
machines. You may get thirsty and
build an appetite with all the jitters
and talking.

3) In Washington State our visit room is
more family friendly then expected,
other families will be in there visiting
their person. The kid's area has
plenty of toys, T. V. and games for
them to enjoy.

4) Be sure your approved on your
persons visiting list before you try
some sneak attack. You would be
heartbroken if you traveled only to be
turned away.

5) Always double check the visiting day you intend on visiting. Sometimes lockdowns, or special events will occur, and visiting will be closed.

6) It's a good idea to discuss whether you might hug or kiss if either is allowed. The less awkward is better for the both of you and your first visit experience.

7) Try and refrain from looking at other people's tables you may see things that could traumatize you, also its bad mojo for your person if you eye gazing other people it's also a sign of respect for your person.

8) Be cordial with the staff but have no intentions on making friends. They

are like FBI agent lurking to take you down.

9) Be prepared for a bit of standoffishness. Some people have gone many years with little to no contact with somebody, it's very common the most neglected are the simple touches. If this is allowed in your facility.

10) For visiting arrivals it's always better to be early then to be late. Sometimes the visiting room will fill up fast and you may have to wait a couple hours for a family to leave.

11) You may feel lots of obsessing over you, eyes all over your body. This is

normal, it's our way of really soaking you up, honestly, it's a good thing.

12) If they have pictures allowed for you and your person you can bet, they will be ready to request a picture of the both of you. Capturing the moment of our first visit with somebody significant is a given.

13) If you are a person who gets overwhelmed with smells, be sure to tell your person not to wear too much cologne very common for guys to overdue it.